THE DOMES OF MARS

BY CASPER BRUNDLE
ILLUSTRATED BY ERIC REESE

PEARSON

Scott
Foresman

Editorial Offices: Glenview, Illinois • Parsippany, New Jersey • New York, New York
Sales Offices: Needham, Massachusetts • Duluth, Georgia • Glenview, Illinois
Coppell, Texas • Ontario, California • Mesa, Arizona

Every effort has been made to secure permission and provide appropriate credit for photographic material. The publisher deeply regrets any omission and pledges to correct errors called to its attention in subsequent editions.

Unless otherwise acknowledged, all photographs are the property of Scott Foresman, a division of Pearson Education.

Illustrations by Eric Reese

Photograph 32 ©DK Images

ISBN: 0-328-13618-2

3 4 5 6 7 8 9 10 V0G1 14 13 12 11 10 09 08 07 06

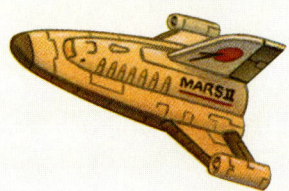

CHAPTER ONE THE DISAPPOINTMENT

"The first thing you must understand," said Captain Fang, "is that life on Mars will be unlike anything that any of you have ever experienced before."

It was silent in the ship's briefing room. Every eye was focused upon the captain's familiar features: his close-cropped silver hair and his wise, blue eyes.

Captain Fang was a tall and physically imposing man. No one knew his exact age, but he was widely believed to be well over a hundred years old. In the last century, scientists had made huge advances in preventing aging, so it was hard to tell.

Captain Fang commanded the attention of everyone in the room. Not one of us would have dared make even the faintest hint of a sound while Fang spoke.

After all, it was far too important a moment. Mars was about to be colonized, and we, the forty men and women (and one dog) assembled in that massive, oval-shaped briefing room, were to be its colonists.

Fang knew he had our complete and undivided attention. It had nothing to do with his rank or age. It was simply a quality that he possessed. It encompassed dignity and authority. Captain Fang was a born leader, and he knew it.

Even if Fang had been the most boring person in the world, we still would have been on the edge of our seats as he spoke. No one had colonized a planet before, let alone Mars. This was an adventure that most of us had been waiting our whole lives to experience.

"Many of you think that our mission will be a grand adventure, and, of course, that's understandable," he said.

He coughed quietly into one hand.

"After all," he continued, "Mars could safely be called uncharted territory. Few humans have traveled there before. Certainly, none have lived there for any length of time. And that, of course, is precisely what we propose to do. We will live there, and I have no doubt that we will survive, thrive, and even flourish."

Some people in the audience nodded at this statement, and a few others smiled.

"So," he continued, "we will be the first. The pioneers of this new frontier. In that sense, yes, our mission will indeed be a grand adventure."

But his expression suggested nothing of the kind. Captain Fang didn't look like a man preparing for any sort of grand adventure. He had neither the flashing eyes, nor the heroic grin of a man who prepares to journey out into the wilderness.

"I am sorry to say that it will be a very dull grand adventure," Fang declared.

Our faces fell. A dull grand adventure? What on Earth was the captain talking about? Some began muttering to each other.

"Yes, that's right," said Fang, beginning to pace as his words came more swiftly. "You heard me right. Because that, my friends, is exactly what life on Mars will be like. At least that's what it will be like in the early days."

"I'm sorry, sir," said a tall fellow with glasses. It was Pietros Giskin, our chief nutritionist and culinary activities specialist. In other words, he was our head cook.

"I don't mean to interrupt," he continued, "but I'm afraid I really don't understand. We're about to become the first humans ever to settle on the red planet and I fail to see how—"

"Mr. Giskin," said the captain, cutting him off neatly.

Giskin swallowed and shrunk in his seat, his face flushing.

"Mr. Giskin," the captain repeated, "you are, of course, quite right. We will become the first humans to colonize Mars, and that is a great achievement."

Giskin nodded vigorously at this.

"We shall doubtless go down in the history books," continued the captain. "And we will, at least in a sense, be saving our people. This is good, important work that we do."

Most of us nodded. After all, this is why we had signed on for the mission. Those of us who had signed on, that is.

"But," the captain added, "there is quite a difference between important work and interesting work."

Sounds of disappointment began to rise from the crew. We hadn't imagined that life on Mars would be easy, but we certainly hadn't anticipated that it might be boring.

"I told you earlier that our existence on Mars will be unlike anything we have experienced before," said the captain, plunging on. "I did not, however, mean this in a strictly positive way. Martian life will be demanding, but not what I'd call interesting. On Mars, you see, we will be challenged by constant extremes. For one thing, there's the temperature."

A willowy blonde woman nodded soberly. She was Ellena Troth, our resident meteorologist.

"It tends to be very cold on Mars," said Fang. "The average temperature hovers around –80°F."

Several of us groaned.

"As I said," Fang continued over the groans, "it tends to be chilly. You can't imagine how cold the Martian winter can be. And it lasts nearly 150 Earth days!"

"And then, there are the dust storms," said the captain as he paced the room again. "They kick up fast, and once they really get going, they blot out everything. You can't see and you certainly can't go anywhere."

"Even in an all-terrain rover?" asked stocky Guy Hercaspian, our security officer.

"Even in an ATR," said Fang. "There would be no visibility, and some Martian storms are strong enough to pick up those little rovers and send them tumbling end over end."

Hercaspian frowned at this. Clearly, nobody had taken the time to tell him about Martian dust storms before we left Earth.

"So," the captain continued, "we will be dealing with subarctic temperatures, highly changeable weather, and powerful dust storms. I haven't even gotten to the potential for quake activity yet."

Another series of groans burst from the crew.

"It may sound dangerous," said Fang, "and it is. It may also sound exciting. However, I'm afraid that this is not the case."

"But why?" asked Hercaspian gloomily.

"Because," said the captain, "we will spend most of our time on Mars sheltered from these dangerous forces. The advance teams have already been there. They've built the domes and installed the atmosphere generators for us. They've even set up an army of servobots, which will help make our stay on Mars much more comfortable. They have taken care of the dangerous part of the assignment. All that remains is the colony-building part."

"But," said Ellena Troth, her face flushing a bit, "I don't see how that could possibly be boring. We'll be paving the way for generations of settlers. We'll be setting up the foundations for what will become a new Martian civilization."

Everyone looked at Ellena and murmured in agreement.

"It's as I said earlier, Ms. Troth," said the captain. "Our mission is important but scarcely interesting. Yes, we'll be accomplishing much of value, but it will hardly be exciting. What it will be is hard work. We'll have to supervise the servobots, build additions to the domes, and handle all mechanical and computer maintenance for the colony. We'll be farmers, construction workers, repair technicians, survivalists, educators, scientists—the list goes on and on."

Fang looked around the room. At the beginning of his speech, all eyes had looked at him in anticipation. Now all he saw was a lot of long faces.

"I'm not telling you this to get you depressed," he said. "I'm not trying to suggest that life on Mars will be unbearable. On the contrary, it will be more than bearable, thanks in part to the servobots waiting on us.

"However," he continued, "I don't want you to land on the red planet with minds still cluttered by daydreams. I don't want you to expect adventure where you will find only monotony."

"Fair enough," said Hercaspian. A thrill seeker, he still appeared to be sulking.

"You are the finest group of colonists the World Council could select," said Captain Fang. "You were chosen from millions of applicants. I know you are up to the challenge. You will be able to handle the hard work, just as you will be able to handle the tedium."

He seemed to take in each one of us. Then he broke into a smile.

"Enough discussion of serious matters," he said. "Our cook servobots have prepared a special feast for us. Let us, as they say, eat, drink, and be merry. Martian thoughts can wait until we arrive on Mars."

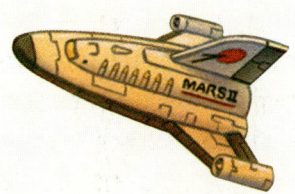

CHAPTER TWO COLONIZING MARS

Once we landed on Mars, I decided that the captain had distorted the truth during his long speech to us.

Certainly, some of what he told us in the ship's briefing room that first day was true. Life on Mars was not as exciting as many of us had expected it to be. At least, it was not interesting initially.

It was not, however, nearly as dull as the captain had warned. Nor was it as free from danger as he had suggested it would be.

I decided, years later, that Fang's intentions in misleading us had been honorable enough. He had hoped to accomplish two chief goals through his speech. First, he wanted to prepare us for the fact that much of Martian life would be dull—rooted in the humdrum and the routine.

Second, he wanted to downplay the severity of the danger we would all be facing. Because there was danger on Mars, to be sure. Mars was the new human frontier. And frontiers, representing the extremities of human experience as they do, always have new and unpredictable dangers.

Like the courageous men and women who had traveled to the frontiers of the American West during the 1800s, we were pioneers. Inevitably, pioneers face threats and hardships. We would be no different. After all, we were living on a new planet, determined to survive in the face of conditions that no Earthling had ever before braved for an extended period of time.

Of course, it wasn't as if we had much choice in the matter. You see, we were fleeing Earth. Or perhaps I should say that we were fleeing what we had done to Earth.

The year was 2204, and Earth was a mess. Humans had depleted most of its natural resources, and nuclear wars had finally devastated the planet. The overuse of oil and other fuels had also taken its toll on Earth's atmosphere. There was no ozone layer left. Now dangerous ultraviolet radiation bombarded the entire planet.

Earth was fast becoming uninhabitable. The remaining population currently survived packed in a series of dingy underground supercities lit by artificial suns. The supercities were all overcrowded, traffic moved at a crawl, families were packed into tiny communal dwellings, and food was always scarce.

That is why the World Council fixed its hopes upon Mars. This was not to say that Mars provided a perfect solution to all of our problems.

Still, it seemed preferable to the alternative: the gradual extinction of the human race and every other living thing on Earth.

The council elders began to look seriously at the colonization of Mars for a number of reasons. First, Mars would be the easiest planet for our star cruisers to reach. The trip would be a long one, but Mars was still the closest planet in the solar system.

Second, Mars's climate was more similar to Earth's climate than any other planet. Venus and Mercury were too given to extremes. Jupiter and the others were simply too far away, not to mention the fact that they are mostly gases.

Only Mars promised temperatures and weather patterns that we could deal with. Even from the beginning, we had understood that we would have to live within enormous protective domes to shield us from the more dangerous elements.

Most importantly, Mars had almost limitless space in which to build new human settlements. There was space that wasn't contaminated by human pollution and carelessness, and we hoped it never would be. The Martian fields of red dust stretched on and on. I had seen pictures of them taken by our satellites. They had an untouched, unique beauty.

There was room for people to build dwellings above and below ground. We had already sent landers to Mars that were not too different from the lunar modules we had used to explore our own moon more than two centuries earlier. So we knew that buried deep below the Martian soil were some of the key minerals and gases that we would need to sustain ourselves and our machines.

But there was still the question of food. The first colonists would start small farms in each of their settlement domes. Each farm would be bathed in sunlight, which would help the crops grow. This light would shine down through special skylights designed to filter out the sun's more harmful rays. There would also be plenty of oxygen for the crops provided by atmosphere generators constructed in each of the domes.

The colonists would also bring a small selection of Earth animals along with them to stock these makeshift farms. These animals would yield a sizeable population of creatures bred to satisfy both our meat and our dairy needs.

There was also the question of water. The World Council's top scientists decided that special water reclamation stations would need to be set up in each dome. These stations would recycle drinkable water from artificial lakes and ponds, thus ensuring that each dome's limited supply of water could be reused.

But the true key to the Martian colony lay in the laws that would guide its workings. The human race had finally learned from its mistakes. Humanity was not about to treat Mars as it had treated Earth.

The Martian colony would be a clean colony. Power would be provided by the sun and not by the messy burning of fuels or dangerous nuclear power.

There would be no pollution to poison what little atmosphere Mars had. The colonists would not be so quick to gobble up the red planet's limited natural resources.

People had also seen just how devastating armed conflict could be. The colonists vowed to coexist peacefully and productively. We would never allow interdome rivalries to turn violent.

Before it even considered selecting a first group of Martian colonists, the World Council decided it would be wise to build a series of colonies for them to live in. So it sent a small group of skilled engineers and environmental specialists to Mars.

This team of twenty men and women stayed on Mars for only a week, but in that time they were able to build five city-sized colonies. They had a little help from robodrone workers, which were made for the purpose of rapid dome construction.

The colony-building operation was a success. The domes were huge, airtight, and even pretty, with gardens and indoor lakes.

But the World Council knew that the next step would be the critical one.

Forty men and women (and a few animals) were selected to be the first Mars colonists. They went through a very tough application process. Many of these applicants were from Eurasia and the Federated States of Africa, but there were also a number from Northeurope, the Americas, and the Kingdom of Antarctica.

Almost everyone on Earth was desperate to leave the planet. Who could blame them? Earth was overcrowded, polluted, and barren. There was little about the planet that one could still love.

But Mars was rich with promise. There was plenty of space, plenty of fresh air (at least in the domes), and plenty of opportunity for advancement.

Many of those who applied to be colonists were idealists eager to save humanity. Many more were just searching for a one-way ticket off the ticking time bomb called Earth.

It was the job of the World Council's selection committee to find those who truly wanted to build a colony. In my opinion they did a great job. The forty selected colonists were fine men and women, and I already thought of them as my new family.

But I would only get a chance to know a few of them. We were divided into separate groups once we arrived on Mars. Eight people (four men and four women) moved into each of the five domes and would live there for a year.

At the end of that year, the World Council would study the data sent back by the colonists and decide if human life on Mars was possible.

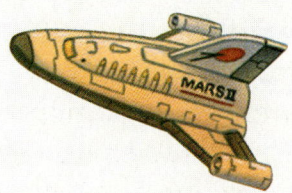

CHAPTER THREE LANDING ON MARS

We landed on Mars after three long, tiring weeks of space travel. We were all glad for a change of scenery. There wasn't much to do aboard a star cruiser, I quickly learned.

In fact, I spent most of the voyage jogging in place on a running strip in our communal fitness center. I also played a few games with gamester servobots. But these robots were older models, and they didn't seem to know any of the games that I liked best. I eventually gave up on them and did my best to find other ways to entertain myself.

When we finally arrived on Mars, I never felt happier to once again set foot on solid ground. Our ship, the *Oregon Trail,* landed at a small spaceport in the Hellas impact basin. The first wave of robodrones had built it for us at roughly the same time the five colony domes were being constructed.

As we glided down into a cavernous underground hangar, a small army of servobots descended upon our ship. They wheeled out several exit ramps and attached them to our ship.

As soon as we stepped down onto the hard concrete floor of the hangar, five tall servobots approached us, hovering on their state-of-the-art antigravity cushions.

"All Dome Alpha settlers," said the first servobot in its lifeless, metallic voice. "All settlers reporting to Dome Alpha, please follow me."

Immediately several members of our group broke away and gathered around the stick-figure-like robot.

Another servobot came forward and called out to the settlers assigned to Dome Beta. Then a third robot did the same, and so on, until we had been divided into five equal groups of colonists.

I was pleased to see that Captain Fang was one of the settlers who reported to Dome Delta with me. So were Ellena Troth, the meteorologist, and Guy Hercaspian, the security officer.

"Is this everyone?" asked the robot.

"Yes," responded Captain Fang. "We're all present and accounted for."

"Very good," said our servobot. "Please take all luggage units and follow me."

Those of us who had suitcases lifted them from the floor. This did not include me since I always travel light. The suitcases contained only a few personal items each. Our heavier, more important cargo would be transported from the ship to the domes by bulky lifter servobots. Then we trotted off after the fast-moving figure of our robot guide.

"What's your name?" asked Harry Fistbern, a former elementary school teacher with dark-tinted glasses. He was an inquisitive fellow whom I liked well enough but for one small problem: his overpowering cologne. I have a very sensitive sense of smell, and I found his scent to border on the unbearable.

"I am called XPG-1045," replied the servobot. "But previous masters have called me Tinny."

"Okay, then, Tinny," said the former schoolteacher. "Where are we heading?"

"We are heading toward an atmospheric shuttle," replied the robot, as it floated swiftly across the spaceport hangar. "It will take us directly to Dome Delta."

"And about how long a trip will that be?" asked Captain Fang.

"Approximately one hour," said Tinny.

"That's a fast shuttle," declared Fang.

"Oh, yes," replied the servobot. "It is very fast. The atmospheric shuttles are the only air traffic on Mars."

The robot glanced at each of us in turn with its glowing red eyes and continued. "As a result each shuttle may travel many times faster than an Earth airplane could without any danger of a midair collision."

"Interesting," said Hercaspian.

"I'll say," agreed Ellena Troth. "It reminds you of just how empty this place is. It's a clean slate—fresh and undisturbed."

"Let's just hope that we can keep it that way," said Captain Fang. He looked seriously at all of us as he climbed onto the waiting shuttle.

Troth nodded gravely as she followed Fang onto the shuttle. But then, just for a fraction of a second, I saw her face distort into a smile. She screwed up her eyes, wrinkled her nose, and stuck out her tongue. The captain was facing the other way and did not see Ellena make a face at him. I decided that I liked this woman very much. Captain Fang could be so serious. It was nice to have someone to lighten the mood.

We all boarded the shuttle, and soon we were zooming off through the Martian skies. A pilot servobot was flying the ship as it soared through majestic canyons and towering mountain ranges.

I stared out the window and soon found myself absorbed by the swirling beauty of a series of dust storms that I could just make out on the horizon. Tinny noticed what I was looking at and turned to address the entire group.

"Do not worry about the Martian dust storms," Tinny told us. "This ship and the other shuttles are outfitted with special cushioning stabilizers. No matter how intense outside conditions may become, no one on board will ever feel anything more than the very slightest swaying motion."

"Now that's a clever idea," remarked Hercaspian.

"It is a necessity, Mr. Hercaspian," said Tinny. "Martian dust storms are fast and unpredictable. It is impossible for even a Grade A pilot servobot to avoid them. Therefore, it was necessary to design a ship that could endure the effects of a dust storm, should it be caught in the middle of one."

"That first group of engineers certainly did their homework," said Troth.

"Actually, Ms. Troth," said Tinny, "the cushioning stabilizers were not designed by human engineers. They were designed by servobots."

This statement took us all by surprise.

"By servobots?" asked Hercaspian in disbelief. "How can that be? I've never heard of servobots designing technology of their own."

"Nevertheless," said Tinny, "it is true. The human engineers who came here to design and build the domes had a very limited amount of time on the planet. It was impossible for them to think of every device that colonists might need."

The robot paused for a moment and then continued.

"They left several specially programmed servobots behind. These servobots were designed to study transportation, farming, and energy-related problems that might arise for colonists, and then to devise solutions."

"Remarkable!" said Troth. "True artificial intelligence!"

"You are too kind," replied Tinny. "I prefer to call it superior programming. Without guidance from humans there is little we servobots can do on our own."

"Still," said Hercaspian, "nice work on the stabilizers. It sounds like they must be real lifesavers."

"Oh, yes," replied Tinny. "I am told that being tossed around by a dust storm aboard an unprotected shuttle can be very distressing to the human digestive system."

"I can imagine it is," said Captain Fang. "Humans can be quite delicate that way."

We were quiet for the remainder of the flight. This gave me plenty of time to stare out the window at the beauty of the Martian landscape.

Red deserts, red mountains, red valleys; I was hypnotized by the never-ending array of reds and browns flashing by outside our ship.

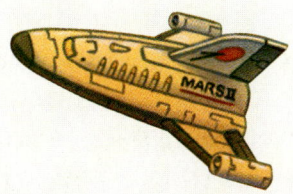

CHAPTER FOUR LIFE IN THE DOME

A little less than an hour later, we arrived at Dome Delta. I was more than a little awed by the sheer size of the facility. I think we all were.

It was roughly the size of five football fields laid end to end, and it was honeycombed by a maze of corridors, chambers, science labs, atmosphere generator rooms, and indoor farms.

There were so many rooms and so much space. And yet, for now, there were fewer than a dozen of us to inhabit the dome.

After enduring the tightly packed supercities of Earth for so long, it felt slightly surreal to be surrounded by so much empty space. I think I felt a little guilty about it too.

Tinny wasted no time leading us on a lengthy, step-by-step tour of the facility. The robot showed us the living quarters and the farming pastures. It showed us movie theaters and storage chambers, swimming pools and artificial lakes. There were parks, streets, and multivehicle garages located beneath the curved arc of a protective dome that shielded us from the thin Martian atmosphere.

Much of the world under the dome was to my liking. I was especially impressed by the garden, which boasted exotic plants that had once grown on Earth. But I still found myself overwhelmed by the grand scale of the place. I felt even smaller than usual.

After Tinny's nearly endless tour of the colony ended, we began moving in and making it our home.

This was easier said than done. The dome was too large, too cold, too impersonal. It didn't feel like any home I had ever known before. I don't think I was the only one having difficulty adjusting either.

For weeks Ellena Troth wandered about looking sickly. Guy Hercaspian, our resident man-of-action, was often sullen and brooding. I wondered if we were suffering from nothing more serious than a case of homesickness.

As time passed and I began to feel better, I decided that I had been right. Homesickness had indeed struck. Earth may have been a miserable place, but it had been the only home we had ever known. It is difficult to leave a place without missing it, even just a little.

It was during those first few weeks at Dome Delta that I began to think about the speech Captain Fang had given aboard the *Oregon Trail.* I decided that the captain had had the right idea.

As soon as the initial excitement wore off, boredom did begin to set in. As Fang had told us, important work isn't always interesting work. And as we shuffled from chamber to chamber, minding the indoor farms and keeping an eye on the atmosphere generators and water tanks, we became increasingly aware of this.

There is nothing interesting about milking cows in the middle of a tiny indoor meadow on Mars. Not that I was actually the one doing the milking, mind you. I wasn't really cut out for that kind of task.

But I watched Bobina Murto, our farming specialist, do so on many occasions. And after watching her do it the first time, what little magic the process may have held definitely wore off.

Few of our other daily tasks were any more interesting. All were necessary—vital, even. From a mission perspective we were progressing by leaps and bounds. We had become entirely self-sufficient. We breathed clean air generated by the atmosphere generators; we drank pure water recycled from the indoor ponds by Donnie Delfino, our water-recycling officer; and we dined on organic greens raised on Dome Delta farms, not to mention fresh cuts of meat from animals housed in the paddocks.

Each day we tested the possibility of long-term Martian living. We performed endless experiments and tests. Captain Fang had already collected a mountain of data on Martian rock formations.

Guy Hercaspian had recovered from his restlessness. Every day he went out in his ATR, exploring the countryside and looking for possible threats to colony security. He seemed desperate to find some sign of life on Mars. So far he had found nothing, much to his obvious disappointment.

Ellena Troth studied the local weather patterns to find out whether or not we would have to modify the domes to protect them from temperature and air-pressure changes.

Donnie Delfino tested the practicality of daily water recycling, and Bobino Murto assessed the effectiveness of indoor Martian farming.

As for me, I did what I always do. I assume that I did it well, because I didn't hear a single complaint from the other settlers.

In fact, I often received some rather nice compliments from several of them. I say this not to brag but to demonstrate that I was thought of as a good fellow and was well liked.

I was particularly pleased to receive one such compliment from Ellena Troth the third week of our stay at Dome Delta. It was dinner time, and I wasn't feeling particularly hungry that night. So I decided to present her with a choice piece of roasted chicken from my plate.

"Sydney!" she said, beaming. "You are so sweet! You are so, so sweet!"

I must confess I blushed a bit at this. It's tough to admit that I blush sometimes. But believe me, I did.

I liked Ellena and was seldom bored in her company. But the rest of the time—well, it's like the captain said. Important things and interesting things are two vastly different concepts. The days passed, and the weeks, and the months. I began to lose track of time.

It was sometime around the beginning of our sixth month at Dome Delta that I learned the captain had not been entirely honest about the absence of danger on Mars. I also learned that things would not always be quite as boring as Fang had led us to believe.

One morning I decided to go with Hercaspian on one of his ATR treks through the Martian terrain. I admit that Ellena Troth had also agreed to go with Hercaspian on his mission that day.

The thought of her alone with that dim-witted (but handsome) Hercaspian made my blood boil. So I insisted that they take me along.

"What is it, Sydney?" Ellena asked me. "I just don't get you at all today."

As we drove along under the glowing red ball of the rising sun, I was delighted to see Hercaspian shoot me several sour looks that he tried to hide from Troth.

About half an hour after we set out, we arrived at a mound of dirt that dwarfed our three-wheeled vehicle. It was shaped like a pyramid and rose nearly fifty feet. As soon as he spotted it, Hercaspian stopped the ATR and frowned.

"That's funny," he said, rubbing his jaw.

"What's funny?" asked Ellena.

"Well," said Hercaspian. "I've come to this spot several times before, and I've never seen that pile of dirt."

"Perhaps it was kicked up by a dust storm," said Ellena. I also thought this was the reason for the sudden mound.

"I don't know," said Hercaspian. "Would a dust storm really create a dirt formation like that? It seems so symmetrical. It doesn't look accidental at all."

Both Ellena and I had to admit that this was true.

"But if it wasn't a dust storm," Ellena began, "are you suggesting that someone—or something—created it?"

"Perhaps," said Hercaspian. He seemed to be getting increasingly excited. "The whole time we've been living here, I have suspected that Mars was inhabited by some form of native intelligence. Maybe this mound is proof!"

This seemed a little far-fetched. Indigenous life on Mars? I really didn't think so. After all, none of our satellites had ever picked up any evidence of life on Mars.

That, in fact, was one of the reasons the World Council had chosen Mars in the first place. It was uninhabited. Humanity had learned its lessons, and it did not want to displace native life forms just to save itself. Humans had done that sort of thing in the past, and it had always had terrible consequences.

The bottom line was that there was really no chance Hercaspian would find native life on Mars. I think Ellena was about to say so as well. But she didn't get the chance. No sooner did she open her mouth to speak than the ground in front of us began to rumble and shake.

"What's that?" asked Troth, peering ahead.

I could feel my stomach sinking. Captain Fang had warned us about the danger of Martian ground quakes. The domes were specially constructed to withstand a quake of any magnitude. But out here, in an unprotected ATR, we were in trouble.

But it wasn't a quake. The soil in front of us rolled and bulged, like the waves of a storm-tossed ocean. We were about to meet our very first native Martian.

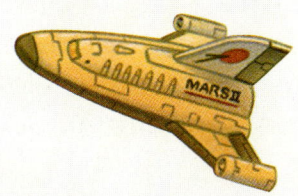

CHAPTER FIVE THE MARTIAN

A massive green and brown creature erupted out of the dirt mound before us, scattering reddish Martian dust this way and that.

It was the scariest beast I had ever seen. The Martian was about a hundred feet long, with a tubular body and rough, scaly skin. It had a wide, circular mouth, ringed by row after row of needlelike teeth. It also had short, pointy tentacles growing out of its sides and huge red eyes located near the front of its face. Thin, flexible stalks stuck out of its head near its eyes.

As it towered over us, the creature made a series of loud, angry noises. These cries made me think of braying donkeys, laughing hyenas, and moaning deep-ocean whales, all rolled together into a single sound. I wished I could cover my ears.

I do not consider myself to be a coward. In fact, on many occasions I have taken pride in my bravery. But at that moment, staring at that wormlike monstrosity, I didn't feel very brave at all. In fact, I felt downright petrified.

I could feel the hair rising on my back. And then, even though I didn't mean to, I began to do what I always do in situations of that kind.

I began to bark.

"Arf!" I said. "Arf, arf, arf, arf, arf!"

"It's okay, boy," said Ellena, reaching over and smoothing down my fur. "It's all right, Sydney."

But I could see that she had turned milky white herself, and I found that I couldn't take much comfort from her soothing words.

Hercaspian's hands tensed on the ATR's steering column. I could see him waiting for the worm-thing to make its first move. For several long, heart-stopping moments, it did nothing. It simply stood there, waving from side to side and staring down at us.

And then, with no warning at all, it came rocketing toward us. That was exactly the cue Hercaspian had been waiting for. He threw the ATR into reverse, spun it around, and took off in the direction we had come from at full speed.

We rocked and jolted across the Martian landscape. But as fast as we were, the worm-thing was faster. I could see in our rearview monitor that it was gaining on us. It was moving its body back and forth across the dust like a snake and approaching at a terrible speed.

I thanked my lucky stars that Hercaspian was such a good driver. We threaded our way between rock formations and bounced across sand dunes. But the worm-thing continued its angry pursuit, and with every second, it seemed to be drawing closer.

"We're not going to make it!" Ellena shouted.

"Yes, we are!" Hercaspian shouted back.

I glanced at the rearview monitor again. The huge worm-thing had nearly caught up with us.

And then suddenly it stopped. Just like that, the worm-thing ground to a halt, and then quickly flipped itself over and slithered off in the opposite direction.

I cannot begin to express the relief that I felt at that moment. And so I decided to give voice to my sentiments.

"Woof!" I said, barking after the retreating worm-thing. I don't normally use such bad language. But I was very upset at the time.

Hercaspian and Ellena were also quite shaken up. Luckily, the security officer was able to muster enough energy to drive us back to Dome Delta.

Once safely inside the dome, we wasted no time telling Captain Fang about the creature we had discovered. Of course, Hercaspian and Ellena did most of the talking, but I occasionally spoke up if I felt that they had missed a particularly important part of the story.

"Arf!" I said, when I realized that they had done a poor job of describing the monster's beady red eyes. "Arf, arf, arf!"

"Yes, boy," said Captain Fang, grinning. "Would you like a treat? Would you? Would you? That's a good boy, Sydney."

"Arf, arf!" I responded. I didn't want a treat. I wanted to describe the worm creature's eyes.

"What a good boy!" said Fang. "What a good boy he is!" And then he gave me a doggie treat.

I decided that being the first dog on Mars wasn't all that I had hoped it would be. But I will confess, the doggie treat was fairly tasty. So the experience wasn't entirely a bad one.

Later Hercaspian and several security officers from the other domes set out in a hover-shuttle to learn more about the worm creatures.

They studied the monsters for days. They observed them from high above, where the worms could not reach them. And they soon learned why the Martian creature had chased us that morning.

The mound, it turned out, was full of eggs. It was some kind of nest. The worm that had chased us was apparently a mother worm.

It didn't really want to eat us. It simply wanted to make sure that we didn't harm its babies.

As weeks went by, and we studied the worms more and more, we discovered that they were very gentle creatures. They were highly social animals and took very good care of their young. The only time they were aggressive was when they felt threatened by intruders.

In the end it was Tinny and his fellow servobots who allowed us to learn more about the worm creatures. We used some of Captain Fang's software to make sense of the worms' language. Then we programmed Tinny and the others so that they could speak it.

None of us could master the language ourselves. Only a robot could make the sounds of wormspeak. Neither human nor canine vocal cords could handle the complexity of their vocal sounds.

Tinny and the other servobots became our ambassadors to the worm creatures. It was thanks to their efforts that a friendship formed between the humans and the worms.

You might be surprised to hear that the worms were only the first of many indigenous life forms we found on the planet. The more creatures we discovered, the more interesting life became.

Our first year on Mars is finally drawing to a close now. The mission has been a success. We have discovered that colonization will be entirely possible.

Not only that, but the worm creatures have announced a willingness to help with our future colony building, as long as we are careful not to intrude upon their underground lairs.

It has been such an eventful year. I could tell you about it for days on end, but I think you have probably heard enough. You can read the rest of the story in Captain Fang's book, *How I Colonized Mars.*

Now, if you will please excuse me, I've got to go. I can hear my master calling. It's time for my dinner. And after that, perhaps a doggie treat. Yes, that would hit the spot, I think.

Mars: Its Weather and Seasons

The weather on Mars is unpredictable. Dust storms arise swiftly. Some Martian dust storms are so large that they cover the equivalent of an entire continent on Earth!

Although Mars is prone to dust storms, it never has rainstorms. This is because there is no liquid water on Mars. However, dry river beds suggest that Mars had water on its surface billions of years ago, when the climate was very different.

By Earth standards, Mars is almost always cold. On an average Martian day, the temperature is −81°F. Temperatures can drop much lower than that and can do so rapidly.

The seasons on Mars are also very different from those on Earth. Mars has seasons that are much longer than Earth seasons. In North America, spring lasts about ninety-three days, summer lasts ninety-four, and fall and winter each last eighty-nine days. In Mars's northern hemisphere, spring and fall last approximately 171 Earth days each, while summer lasts 199 Earth days and winter lasts 146 Earth days.